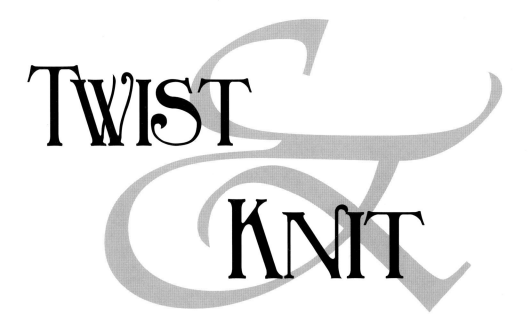

TWIST & KNIT

A Dozen Knitted Patterns
for Handspun, Hand-dyed
and One-of-a-kind Yarns

Miriam L. Felton

Twist & Knit: A Dozen Knitted Patterns for Handspun, Hand-dyed, and One-of-a-kind Yarns

ISBN 978-0-9792017-3-8

Published by: Cooperative Press,
13000 Athens Ave C288
Lakewood Ohio 44107
http://www.cooperativepress.com
info@cooperativepress.com

Author: Miriam L. Felton
Photography & Book Design: Miriam L. Felton in Salt Lake City, Utah, USA

First Printing: July 2010
Printed & Bound in Salt Lake City, Utah, USA by Artistic Printing Company

Layout and Pre-Press in Scribus, a free open-source desktop publishing program. www.scribus.net

The body copy of this book is in **Gentium Book Basic**
Patterns and tutorials are in **Century Gothic**
Headings and titles are in BIRMINGHAM

Knitting Charts were created in Knit Visualizer. www.knitfoundry.com

FOR CALEB

FOR EVER AND ALWAYS

MY SUPPORT, MY JOY, & MY LOVE

ACKNOWLEDGMENTS

For the last year, this book has been a wonder, a joy, and a pain in the arse, but I would be remiss if I let this opportunity pass without thanking the people who kept me focused, helped me keep my wits, and reminded me that everything would be alright.

To my large and ever-expanding family, and to my knitting friends - Anne Podlesak, Ysolda Teague, Margene Smith, Nancy Bush, Teri Shea, Shannon Okey, Marge Yee-Norrander and Annie Modesitt - my most heartfelt thanks for your support, encouragment and belief in my abilities.

A special thank you to my Sample Knitters and Spinners- Cathy Arfin, Lauren Lax, Anne Podlesak, Rhonna Robbins-Sponaas, Margene Smith, and Marge Yee-Norrander. Without you it would have taken twice as long to finish this book.

Eternal thanks to Kristi Porter, tech editor extraordinaire.

These pages would be much dimmer were it not for the modeling acumen and enthusiastic participation of my friend Paige Pitcher.

Thanks to Cat Bordhi and her Visionary Group for proving that self published books could be done, and done well.

This book rings true.

TABLE OF CONTENTS

Introduction. 1

Notes on Gauge. 1

Supplies. 2

Special Techniques. 5

Yarn & Fiber Resources. 6

Accessory Resources. 7

Abbreviations & Chart Legend. 8

Yarn Weight Reference Chart. 10

Reading Charts. 11

Tutorials
　　Casting On Over Two Needles. 12
　　Provisional Cast-On. 14
　　Disappearing Loop Cast-On. 16
　　Double Stranded Double-Start Cast-On. 18
　　Knitted Lace Bind-Off. 22
　　Purled Lace Bind-Off. 24
　　Stretchy Sewn Bind-Off. 26
　　Make 5 Sts Into 1. 28
　　PKOK. 30
　　Blocking. 32

Patterns
　　Dropleaf Wrap. 38
　　Comfy Shawl. 42
　　Vinca Shawl. 46
　　Transverse Scarf. 50
　　Motte Shawl. 54
　　Porifera Socks. 58
　　Cleite Shawl. 62
　　Lune Shawl. 66
　　Tudor Stole. 70
　　Windward Cowl. 76
　　Colonnade Scarf. 80
　　Gable Mitts 84

Introduction

Every knitter knows the frustration of running out of yarn. This nagging fear is compounded when the yarn is one-of-a-kind or hand-dyed, and simply heartbreaking when you've spent hours spinning the yarn yourself. This book offers twelve patterns specifically designed to get the most out of your unique yarn. All of the patterns have small repeats, very flexible gauge, or carefully selected construction to allow you to use every yard of yarn without sacrificing style or wearability.

Notes on Gauge

Most of these designs (with the exception of the Gable Mitts) can be worked in any weight of yarn. Because of this, knitting a swatch is the best way to know what your finished piece will be like ahead of time. When you swatch, try a few different needle sizes and make sure you wash and block your swatches.

Choosing a needle size can be tricky for lace, but a good place to start is with a needle two sizes larger than the recommended needle for that weight of yarn, i.e. For DK weight yarn, the normal recommened needle size is a US 6 (4 mm), so for lace I would suggest bumping up to a US 8 (5 mm) to swatch. If you like the drape and the openness of the fabric (referred to as the "hand") then go with it. The nice thing about these flexible accessory pieces is that they don't have to fit a certain bust or hip measurement. If a scarf is 4 inches longer than planned it isn't a problem whereas a sweater with 4 inches extra ease is a disaster.

Measuring gauge in lace can be difficult because there is so much movement in the stitches. Also, portions of the lace that have more yarnovers can have a different gauge than pieces that are more solid. The openness of knitted lacey fabric also means that its gauge can be manipulated with blocking. If you need the piece to be narrower, you can block it longer to take up the width and vice versa, as illustrated in this image. It is the same swatch, blocked wide and then blocked long.

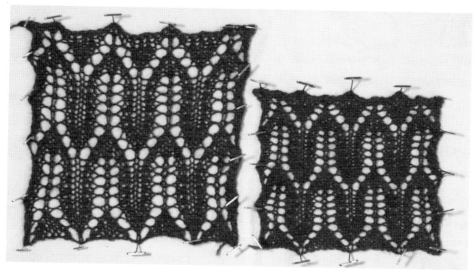

Needle size can greatly effect what your lace looks like. If you want lace with strong lines and a clear distinction between solid and open fabric, go with a relatively smaller needle size (like the swatch on the right). If you want a more open and drapey fabric, go with a relatively larger needle size (like the swatch on the left).

Supplies

The most important part of any knitting project is **the yarn**. Choose a yarn to suit your purpose, i.e. if you are knitting a sweater for a baby, use a machine washable yarn. Try to stick with natural fiber yarns, as they block most effectively. Some man-made fiber content is acceptable, but it can compromise the blockability of the finished piece. Natural fibers include wool, alpaca, llama, angora, mohair, cashmere and silk. Man-made fibers include acrylic, microfiber, acetate, viscose, nylon, polyester and rayon. While cotton is also a natural fiber, it doesn't hold blocking as well as animal-based fibers do. There are many ways to measure the weight of a yarn, most of which are subjective, but some general guidelines about yarn weight can be found on page 10.

Scrap yarn is needed for provisional cast ons. For this purpose, I suggest using something smooth, round and relatively hard like crochet cotton. Crochet cotton comes in many different weights, but something close to the weight of your yarn is best. Since it can also be used for blocking (see page 32) it's a very useful tool to have and cheaper than most yarns. I suggest you get a light or undyed color so it doesn't accidentally bleed onto the rest of your project.

Knitters today are blessed with a wide variety of **needles** to suit every individual taste or project. For lace, it's usually best to have a needle that has a long, sharp point on it. Needles that are too blunt can make some lace decreases difficult to work. All materials (wood, acrylic, or metal) will work equally well depending on your tension and knitting style. Wood and bamboo needles tend to grip the stitches a bit better, while metal needles usually are slick and allow the stitches to move more freely. If you are a loose knitter, you may prefer the grippy surface of bamboo, or if you are a fast knitter, you may prefer the slick surface of metal. Find the needle type that works best for you.

When a piece is worked flat you can use either circular needles or straight needles, but when you have an increasing number of stitches—as in a top-down triangle or circular shawl (such as Cleite or Lune)—the vast number of stitches for the latter part of the shawl won't fit on a straight needle very well. In these cases a circular is preferred because the stitches can bunch up on the cable. They can't bunch up as compactly on a straight needle. More stitches will fit on a circular needle vs. a straight needle of the same length.

Stitch Markers can be very useful. They sit on your needles between stitches and remind you to work a decrease, mark chart repeats, or serve as an aid for counting your stitches. They are simply slipped from the left-hand needle to the right-hand needle when you come to them. Sometimes a pattern's decreases need to be worked with stitches on both sides of a marker. If this is the case, I've included a note in the individual pattern to indicate this fact. If you find that markers are slowing you down or getting in your way, feel free to remove them. All patterns can be worked without markers if preferred, but if you are new to lace or cannot yet read your knitting, the markers between repeats may help.

Some patterns will tell you to weigh your yarn. For this you will need access to a **scale**. A typical food scale is not accurate enough for use in this instance. I would suggest a digital scale, with gram measurements, which can usually be purchased for less than $20 USD. It doesn't need a high maximum capacity, since the chances you're working with more than two pounds of yarn are slim. If you have the option, gram measures with decimal points can be very helpful. If you can't invest in a digital scale, most yarn stores have one and will be happy to let you use it, but it doesn't hurt to ask ahead just in case.

Some patterns suggest that you work from both ends of the ball. In order to make this possible, you will need a ball from which you can pull 2 strands -- from the center and the outside. A standard **ball winder** will supply such a ball, but you can wind a centerpull ball on your thumb or any similar long tube. A **nostepinne** is a wooden tool specifically for winding centerpull balls.

After carrying your knitting around for weeks, it will definitely need a bath when it's bound off. A good quality **rinse-free wash** can clean your yarn, soften the fabric, and make it smell lovely. I do not recommend the standard "wool washes" that you get in a grocery store, they are not actually formulated to be good for wool, and they do need rinsing. The more times you have to rinse your knitting, the more likely it is you will accidentally felt it. You can find a variety of rinse-free washes in myriad scents carried in any local yarn store. Some names to look for are **SOAK** and **Eucalan**.

Blocking equipment is also very important when you're trying to get the most area out of limited knitting, and is absolutely essential to lace. Blocking can be done on the cheap with cotton crochet thread, but if you're planning on doing more than a few scarves or lace pieces in your lifetime, it's worth it to have quality materials. See page 32 for detailed blocking instructions.

Pins are absolutely essential. Any strong, sturdy pins will work, but T-Pins will save your fingertips from much pain if you're pinning out a large piece. Most yarn stores carry small quantities of T-Pins, but check drapery suppliers or home decor places for large quantities, often sold by the pound.

Blocking wires will help you get a straight or curved edge (as in the Lune shawl). My blocking wires are 16 gauge stainless steel welding rods, housed in a PVC pipe with screw-on end caps. I paid about $20 for 32 rods (purchased by the pound at a welding supply store), and sold off the extras to local knitters. If you go this route, PLEASE remember to ask for stainless steel rods. Non-stainless rods will react with water in the knitted fabric when you block, creating rust where the rods touch the wet knitting. You would be left with rust stained knitting when the blocking is done. This is why it is so important to get stainless steel rods.

Special Techniques

To get the most knitted fabric from your yarn, there are a few techniques with which you will need to become familiar. The first is how to weigh your yarn. Some patterns in this book require that you split your yarn in half. For some items (such as the Porifera Socks or Gable Mitts), you can work from both ends of a center pull ball at once. But for a piece like Vinca, it's beneficial to have two separate balls, each with half of the yarn when you split for the wings. To do this, when you reach the point in the pattern where you need to split your yarn, weigh the full ball and record how much yarn you have total. Place your scale on the floor by your ball-winder and begin winding, keeping the digital scale on. The scale will read less and less as you wind off yarn from the full ball.

When the scale reads half of the total yarn weight, mark that point in your yarn (a slip knot with a bobby pin or paper clip through the loop works really well). Remove the ball from the ball winder and weigh both balls separately to make sure that they are equal. If not wind a few yards from the larger ball to the smaller and weigh again. When you're satisfied you've got two equal balls, break the yarn and continue with the pattern as instructed.

Another technique that will become invaluable is how to measure how much yarn you are using per row or round. Once you've finished a row/round, measure off a yard of yarn from the piece. Tie a slip knot at this point and and put something through the loop of the slip knot (like a safety pin, or bobby pin). This keeps the slip knot from becoming unknotted as you put tension on the yarn. Work one row/round. Measure from your knitting to the slip knot. Subtract that distance from the 1 yard you measured, and you have determined how much yarn you used in a round.

If you reach the slip knot before finishing the row/round, remove the slip knot, finish the row/round, and start the process again, but this time, measure off two or three yards before the slip knot and knit a row/round and measure how much you have left.

Most of the pieces require you to leave a certain length of yarn in reserve for the bind off (i.e. 4 rows worth of yarn). This is when it becomes essential to know how much yarn you use per row/round. Also, if you need to finish your knitting on a certain row of the chart to complete a repeat, then you can determine if you have enough yarn left to finish another repeat by using this method.

Yarn & Fiber Resources

Thank you to all the yarn and fiber companies who supplied the materials used in this book:

Berroco
Yarn: Ultra Alpaca Fine
PO Box 367
Uxbridge, Massachusetts, USA, 01569
http://www.berroco.com

Cascade
Yarn: Ecological Wool
http://www.cascadeyarns.com/

Chameleon Colorworks
http://www.chameleoncolorworks.com/

Green Mountain Spinnery
Yarn: New Mexico Organic
P.O. Box 568
Putney, Vermont, USA, 05346
http://www.spinnery.com

Habu Textiles
Yarn: N-6B Konnyaku Sizing Silk
135 W. 29th Street, Suite 804
New York, New York, USA, 10001
http://www.habutextiles.com

Kelbourne Woolens
Yarn: The Fibre Company Canopy Fingering
915 N 28th Street, 2nd Floor
Philadelphia, Pennsylvania, USA 19130
http://www.kelbournewoolens.com

Lorna's Laces
Yarn: Pearl
4229 North Honore St
Chicago, Illinois, USA, 60613
http://www.lornaslaces.net

Malabrigo
Yarn: Merino Lace
http://www.malabrigoyarn.com

Peace Fleece
Yarn: Peace Fleece Worsted
475 Porterfield Road
Porter, Maine, USA, 04068
http://www.peacefleece.com

Red Rocks Fiber Works
Yarn: Steamboat
Denver, Colorado, USA
http://redrocksfiberworks.com

Spinderella's
Fiber: Thrums
1640 South 600 East
Salt Lake City, Utah, USA, 84105
http://www.spinderellas.com

Spirit Trail Fiberworks
Fiber: 50/50 Merino Silk Top
PO Box 197
Sperryville, Virginia, USA, 22740
http://www.spirit-trail.net

Spritely Goods
Yarn: Sylph
http://www.spritelygoods.com

Spunky Eclectic
Fiber: Almost Solid BFL Roving & Panda Roving
http://www.spunkyeclectic.com

Sundara Yarn
Yarn: Silk Lace
http://www.sundarayarn.com

Woolen Rabbit
Yarn: Harmony Sock
PO Box 1415
Conway, New Hampshire, USA, 03818
http://www.thewoolenrabbit.com

Wooly Wonka Fibers
Fiber: Superfine Merino
White Rock, New Mexico
http://www.woolywonkafiber.com

Accessory Resources

Oak Leaf Shawl Pin & Swirl Penannular
Designs by Romi
http://designsbyromi.com

Ethereal Over the Knee Socks
Sock Dreams
Portland, Oregon, USA
http://www.sockdreams.com

Filigree Stick Pin
Leslie Wind
http://www.lesliewind.com

Chart Symbol	Abbreviation	Directions: RS (Right Side)	WS (Wrong Side)
☐	k	Knit stitch	Purl stitch
B	ktbl	Knit stitch through back loop	Purl stitch through back loop
●	p	Purl stitch	Knit Stitch
(grey box)	No Stitch	There is no stitch here. This is a placeholder allowing the chart to be square. Move past all "No Stitch" boxes without altering your knitting.	There is no stitch here. This is a placeholder allowing the chart to be square. Move past all "No Stitch" boxes without altering your knitting.
V	sl wyib	Slip 1 st with the working yarn held in the back	Slip 1 st with the working yarn held in the front
O	yo	Yarn over	Yarn over
②	yo2	yarn over twice	Yarn over twice
M	m1	Make one by lifting strand in between stitch just worked and the next stitch, knit into the back of this thread so that the stitch is twisted.	Make one by lifting strand in between stitch just worked and the next stitch, purl into back of this thread so that the stitch is twisted.
V⁵	m5 sts in 1	(K1, yo, k1, yo, k1) into one stitch	(P1, yo, p1, yo, p1) into one stitch
⑂	kf&b	Knit into front loop of stitch without removing it from the left hand needle. Knit into back loop of stitch, then drop off left-hand needle.	No WS definition required.
＼	ssk	Slip one stitch as if to knit, slip another stitch as if to knit. Insert left-hand needle into front of these 2 stitches and knit them together	Purl two stitches together in back loops, inserting needle from the left, behind and into the backs of the 2nd & 1st stitches in that order.
／	k2tog	Knit two stitches together as one stitch	Purl two stitches together as one stitch
＼ (barred)	k2tog tbl	Knit two stitches together through back loops	Purl two stitches together through back loops, inserting needle from the left, behind and into the backs of the 2nd and 1st stitches in that order.
⟋	k3tog	Knit three stitches together as one	Purl three stitches together as one
＼	k3tog tbl	Knit three stitches together through back loops.	Purl three stitches together as one, inserting needle from the left and behind.
⋏	sl1 k2tog psso	Slip 1, k2tog, pass slipped stitch over k2tog	No WS definition required.
⋀	CDD	Central Double Decrease – Slip first and second stitches together as if to knit. Knit 1 stitch. Pass two slipped stitches over the knit stitch.	Central Double Decrease – Slip first and second stitches together as if to purl through the back loop. Purl 1 stitch. Pass two slipped stitches over the purl stitch.
⟋.	p2tog	Purl two stitches together as one	Knit two stitches together as one

Chart Symbol	Abbreviation	Directions:	
		RS (Right Side)	WS (Wrong Side)
⌐⎹O⌐	pkok	Pass third stitch in on the left hand needle over the previous two and drop off the needle. K1, yo, k1.	No WS definition required.
(symbol)	c2 over 2 left	Slip 2 sts to cable needle, hold in front. Knit 2, then knit 2 from cable needle.	No WS definition required.
(symbol)	c2 over 2 right	Slip 2 sts to cable needle, hold in back. Knit 2, then knit 2 from cable needle.	No WS definition required.
(symbol)	Left Twist	Slip 1 st to cable needle, hold in front. K1, then k1 from cable needle.	No WS definition required.
(symbol)	Right Twist	Slip 1 st to cable needle, hold in back. K1, then k1 from cable needle.	No WS definition required.
(symbol)	1/1 right cross PB	Slip 2 sts to cable needle, hold in back. K1, slip center st from cable needle back to left hand needle and purl it. K1 from cable needle.	No WS definition required.
(symbol)	1/1 left cross PB	Slip 2 sts to cable needle, hold in front. K1, slip center st from cable needle back to left hand needle and purl it. K1 from cable needle.	No WS definition required.
	sl	slip	
	wyif	with yarn in front	
	wyib	with yarn in back	
	pu	pick up	
	pm	place marker	
	sl m	slip marker	
	rnd(s)	round(s)	
	st(s)	stitch(es)	
	yd(s)	yard(s)	
	oz	ounce(s)	
	gm(s)	gram(s)	
	rep	repeat	
	RS	Right Side	
	WS	Wrong Side	
	MC	Main Color	
	CC	Contrasting Color	
	wpi	Wraps per inch – a measurement to determine the weight of a yarn. How many times the yarn can be wrapped around a ruler or a wpi gauge within a one inch space	
	beg	beginning	

	LACE	FINGERING	SPORT	DK	WORSTED	ARAN	CHUNKY	BULKY
aka	aka cobweb and gossamer for the lighter lace weights	aka Sock, 4-ply,	aka Baby, Heavy Fingering	aka Light Worsted, Double Knitting, 8-ply	aka Afghan, 10-ply	aka Heavy Worsted, 12-ply	aka Bulky, Craft, Rug	aka Super-Bulky, Roving, Polar
Symbol	0 LACE	1 SUPER FINE	2 FINE	3 LIGHT	4 MEDIUM	4 MEDIUM	5 BULKY	6 SUPER BULKY
wpi	21 wpi or more	18 - 20 wpi	15 - 17 wpi	12 - 14 wpi	10 - 11 wpi	8 - 9 wpi	7 - 8 wpi	6 wpi or less
sts per inch	8.5 per inch (2.5 cm) or less	7 - 8 sts per inch (2.5 cm)	6 - 7 sts per inch (2.5 cm)	5.5 - 6 sts per inch (2.5 cm)	4.75 - 5.25 sts per inch (2.5 cm)	4 - 4.5 sts per inch (2.5 cm)	2.75 - 3.75 sts per inch (2.5 cm)	2.5 sts per inch (2.5 cm) or less
yards per 50 gm	275 yards or more per 50 gm (1.75 oz) ball	185 - 230 yards per 50 gm (1.75 oz) ball	145 - 180 yards per 50 gm (1.75 oz) ball	120 - 142 yards per 50 gm (1.75 oz) ball	100 - 120 yards per 50 gm (1.75 oz) ball	85 - 100 yards per 50 gm (1.75 oz) ball	70 - 85 yards per 50 gm (1.75 oz) ball	60 yards or less per 50 gm (1.75 oz) ball
yards per 100 gm	545 yards or more per 100 gm (3.5 oz) ball	370 - 460 yards per 100 gm (3.5 oz) ball	290 - 360 yards per 100 gm (3.5 oz) ball	240 - 284 yards per 100 gm (3.5 oz) ball	200 - 240 yards per 100 gm (3.5 oz) ball	170 - 200 yards per 100 gm (3.5 oz) ball	140 - 170 yards per 100 gm (3.5 oz) ball	120 yards or less per 100 gm (3.5 oz) ball
Needle Size	Needle Size smaller than US 1 (2.25mm)	Needle Size US 1 - 3 (2.25 - 3.25mm)	Needle Size US 3 - 5 (3.25 - 3.75mm)	Needle Size US 5 - 6 (3.75 - 4mm)	Needle Size US 7 - 8 (4.5 - 5mm)	Needle Size US 8 - 9 (5 - 5.5mm)	Needle Size US 10 -11 (6 - 8mm)	Needle Size 13 (9mm) and up
For lace	For lace: US 2 - 4 (2.75 - 3.5mm)	For lace: US 4 - 6 (3.5 - 4mm)	For lace: US 5 - 7 (3.75 - 4.5mm)	For lace: US 7 - 9 (4.5 - 5.5mm)	For lace: US 9 - 10 (5.5 - 6mm)	For lace: US 10 - 11 (6 - 8mm)	For lace: US 13 - 15 (9 - 10mm)	For lace: US 15 - 17 (10 - 12 mm) and up.

Yarns show actual size.

Reading Charts

Charts are merely a pictorial representation of the same knitting stitches you find in a text pattern. There are many advantages to using charts. First, they take up less space - a whole large shawl can be charted on only a few pages. Second, with practice it is easier to find your place. When you learn to 'read your stitches' you will begin to be able to see where you are on the chart without having to mark your place.

Figure 1

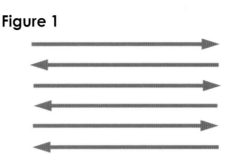

The act of flat knitting is generally done from right to left. We begin at the right-most edge of the knitting and work across to the left-most edge, then flip to the wrong side and do the same. If you were to trace the line of the yarn as it goes from row to row it would look something like figure 1.

If we overlayed that onto a chart, it would look like figure 2:

Figure 2

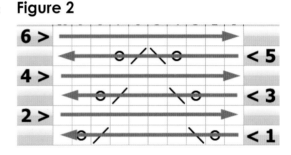

Right side rows are shown as they are intended to be knit, from right to left. But wrong side rows are shown from left to right, which is how they would look if you were only viewing them from the right side of the work. This means that some interpretation is needed to work complicated wrong side rows. In the abbreviations on pages 8 & 9 you will see instructions for a symbol on both RS and WS to help facilitate this interpretation. For most flat knitting charts, right side rows are odd numbers and wrong side are even numbers. If you are working a chart in the round, every row is a right side row, so all rows would be worked from right to left.

If you were to translate a knitting chart box by box you would find that the written instructions would be the same. For example:

Working from right to left (because it is an odd numbered Right Side row), this row translates to k1, yo, ssk, k4, k2tog, yo, k1.

Knowing that an ssk is a left leaning decrease, a k2tog is a right leaning decrease and a yo makes a hole, you can begin to see how easy it is to translate a chart into the stitch by stitch instructions in your head. If you were to knit this row of charted knitting, the yarnovers would look like the circle holes and the decreases would look like slanted lines that you see in the pictorial version.

Charts will often have borders around certain areas to mark repeats. The sections within the borders function the same way as parentheses do in a text pattern.

Stitches that use more than one stitch in their execution will cover more than one box. This cable, for instance, uses 4 stitches to execute (2 to be held in back and 2 held in front), so it covers 4 squares of the chart.

CASTING ON OVER TWO NEEDLES

This cast on is basically the same as a standard long-tail cast on, but worked over two needles.

It creates a wonderfully stretchy and flexible cast on, good for ribbing, lace or anything where you don't want the cast on to restrict the stretch of the fabric.

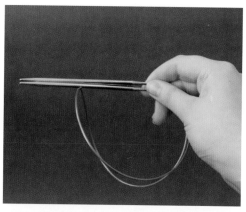

Step 1: Hold two needles together. If you are using a circular needle, hold both ends of the circular together to get the same effect. Make a long tail by wrapping your working yarn around the doubled needle once for every stitch you need to cast on. Add a few inches for good measure and then tie a slip knot between your tail and the rest of the working yarn.

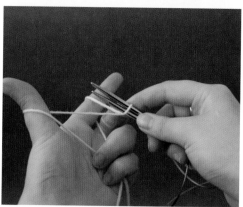

Step 2: Place the slip knot on the doubled needles. With the long tail strand in the back, grab both strands with your back fingers and slip your index finger and thumb between them. Spread your index finger and thumb out, making a V with the yarn tails.

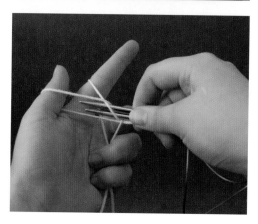

Step 3: Using both needles in unison as if they were one needle, slide the needles under the strand that crosses your thumb.

Loop the needles over and behind the strand on your index finger, pulling up a new loop from the index finger strand.

Drop your thumb loop.

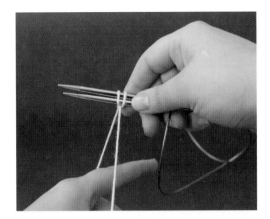

Step 4: Pull down the tails to snug up your new stitch.

Repeat Step 3 & 4 until you have the required number of stitches.

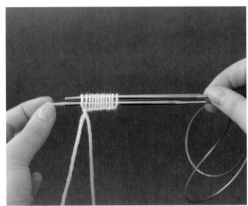

Step 5: Grab the tip of the bottom needle and the end of the top needle and pull them to separate, making sure that the stitches stay on the bottom needle.

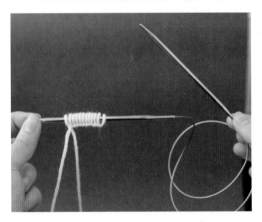

Step 6: Once the top needle is completely removed, you'll have nice loose stitches

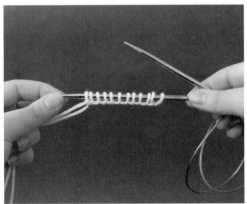

Step 7: As you can see, the stitches will stretch to a normal knitting width very easily. It will also make knitting the first row substantially easier than if you cast on over one needle.

PROVISIONAL CAST-ON

Step 1: With appropriate waste yarn (see page 2) and a crochet hook, begin with a slip knot and place it on the hook.

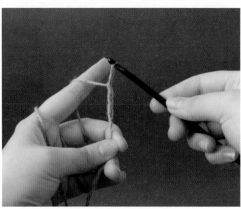

Step 2: Chain a few times by wrapping the yarn over the hook and pulling up a new loop through the loop that was on the hook previously.

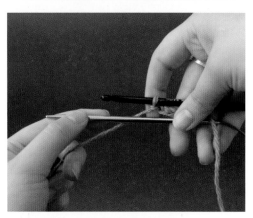

Step 3: Hold your knitting needle parallel to the hook, with the crochet chain held between the hook and needle. Bring the waste yarn behind the needle.

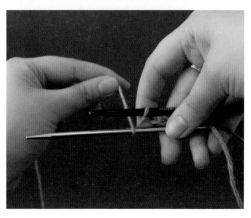

Step 4: Bring the waste yarn between the needle and the hook from front to back.

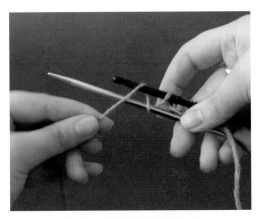

Step 5: Bring the waste yarn over the top of the hook.

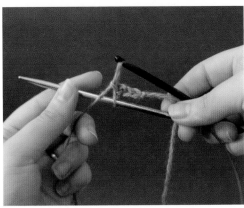

Step 6: Pull the new strand of yarn through the old loop on the hook, creating one provisional stitch on the knitting needle with the chain loop still held between needle and hook.

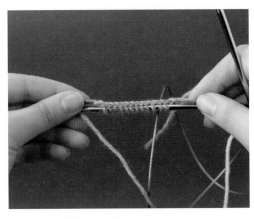

Step 7: Repeat Steps 3-6 until you have the required number of provisional stitches on the needle, then chain a few more times to give another tail. This second tail will give you a buffer when you are ready to unzip the provisional cast-on. You may wish to make it longer than the other tail so you will know which end to begin with when you are unzipping the provisional cast-on.

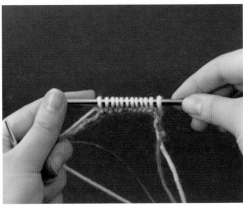

Step 8: Twist the provisional stitches so that the chain sits underneath your knitting needle and knit or purl a row with your working yarn. This will get your working yarn onto the needles so you can begin your pattern. If you begin working patterning using the waste yarn stitches, it will make picking up live stitches very difficult.

Disappearing Loop Cast-On

This cast on creates a snug, close-fitting beginning for circular knitting.

Try to keep your stitches tight against the needle to keep the newly cast on stitches from being sloppy. This will also help keep your double points in place as you work the first few rows.

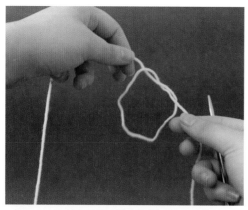

Step 1: Using your working yarn, tie an overhand knot and hold it with the tail end hanging down to the right. Keep the knot open and loose, formed into a circle.

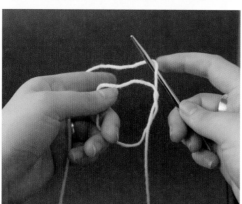

Step 2: Wrap your yarn over the needle from front to back. This is your first stitch.

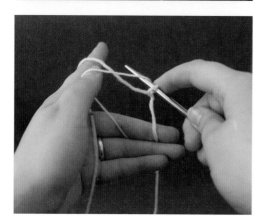

Step 3: Stick your needle through the circle from front to back.

Step 4: Pick up a loop from the yarn closest to the ball and pull it through the circle. This is your second stitch.

Step 5: Yarn over from front to back. This is your third stitch.

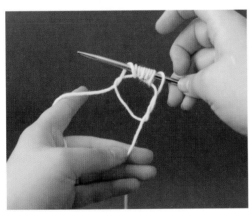

Step 6: Repeat Steps 3-5 until you have the required number of stitches on the needle.

Step 7: Pull the short tail end of the loop and the loop will disappear. Stitches can then be transferred onto multiple double pointed needles, or you can knit the first row, as you would an i-cord, and then transfer to double points.

Double Stranded Double-Start Cast On

The stitches of this cast on are created in pairs. Part 1 creates the first stitch in the sequence, and Part 2 creates the second stitch.   This method creates a beautifully decorative edge. It can be worked with only one strand in the front instead of the doubled strand; for a very open fabric, you could work each pair of stitches as one instead of individually to give a stretchier edge.

I first saw this cast-on used in Nancy Bush's Knitting On the Road from Interweave Press-2001.

Part 1

Step 1: Fold your tail end so that the yarn is doubled for about 2 feet (61 cm). Tie a slip knot in the doubled yarn leaving a tail about 6 inches (15 cm) long This will give you 3 tails, one that is double thick, one short single thick tail, and one single-thick tail attached to your yarn source.

Place the slip knot on the needle in your right hand.

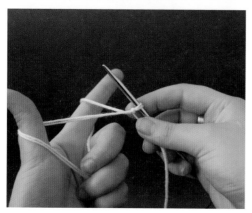

Step 2: With the doubled strand held in front and the single strand in back, grab both strands with your back fingers and slip your index finger and thumb between them. Spread your index finger and thumb out, making a V with the yarn tails.

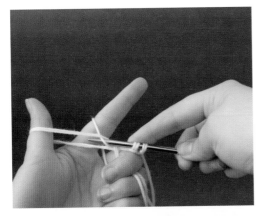

Step 3: Slide the needle under the strand that crosses your thumb

Then loop the needle over and behind the strand on your index finger.

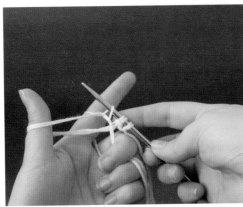

Step 4: Pull up a new loop from the index finger strand.

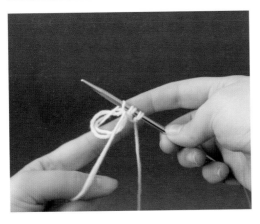

Step 5: Drop your thumb loop and pull down the tails to snug up your new stitch.

Continue to Part 2 on next page

Step 6: Reverse the loop on your thumb so that the strand flows from the needle around the thumb on the side closest to you, then down to join the index-finger strand.

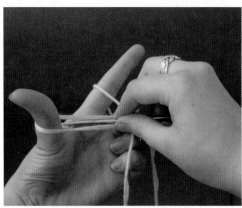

Step 7: Insert the needle through the thumb loop from the tip of the thumb toward your palm.

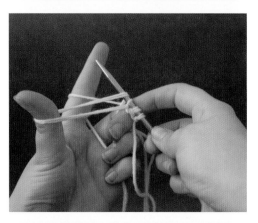

Step 8: Loop the needle over and behind the strand on your index finger.

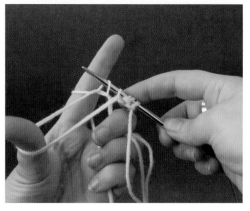

Step 9: Pull up a new loop from the index finger strand.

Step 4: Drop your thumb loop and pull down the tails to snug up your new stitch.

Repeat Steps 2-10 until all required stitches have been cast on.

Knitted Lace Bind Off

This bind off takes about 3 times as much yarn to work than a traditional bind off, but it creates a stretchy edge that is ideal for lace knitting.

Knitting of two stitches together serves to anchor each stitch as it is decreased.

Step 1: Knit two stitches individually.

Step 2: Insert your left-hand needle into the front of these two stitches.

Step 3: Knit them together through the back loop.

Step 4: Knit 1, giving you two stitches on your right-hand needle.

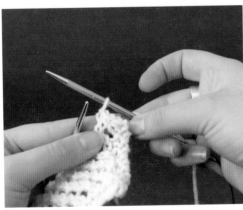

Step 5: Repeat Steps 2-4 until only one loop remains. Break yarn and pull tail end through the final loop

Purled Lace Bind Off

This bind off takes about 3 times as much yarn to work as a traditional bind off, but it creates a stretchy edge that is ideal for lace knitting.

Purling two stitches together serves to anchor each stitch as it is decreased.

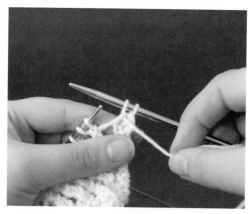

Step 1: Purl two stitches individually.

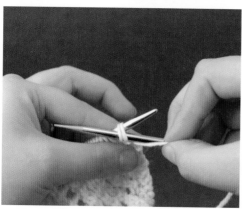

Step 2: Insert your left-hand needle into the back of these two stitches.

Step 3: Purl them together.

Purl 1 more stitch so you have 2 sts on the right hand needle.

Step 4: Repeat Steps 2-3 until only one loop remains. Break yarn and pull tail end through the final loop.

Note: If you knit continental style (with your yarn in your left hand) and use the technique called a Norwegian Purl—purling without bringing the yarn to the front of the work—this bind off will not work for you. I suggest that you work an extra row in the border pattern and then bind off on the following row with a knitted lace bind off (see page 22).

STRETCHY SEWN BIND OFF

This bind off creates a stretchy edge that blends beautifully into ribbing or other stretchy knitted fabrics.

Each stitch is worked 3 times with a blunt needle. As you get more proficient at it, your tension will be more even, and you will find the right snugness to get enough stretch without a loose bind off.

Step 1: Cut a tail of yarn that is 3-4 times as long as the edge to be bound off. If you're binding off ribbing, use the stretched ribbing measurement to estimate the tail.

Thread the tail on to a blunt tapestry needle. One with a bent tip works best.

Step 2: Sew through the first two stitches as if to purl and pull the extra yarn through. Pull it snug, but not tight.

Step 3: Sew back through the first stitch as if to knit and pull the extra yarn through.

Step 4: Remove the first stitch from the needle and drop it.

Step 5: Repeat Steps 2-4 until only one loop remains. Pull tail end through the final loop.

Make 5 sts into 1

Step 1: Work in pattern to the point where you will be working the m5 sts into 1. It will usually be the center of a motif. This is your base stitch.

Step 2: Knit into the base stitch, but do not remove it from the left hand needle.

Step 3: Pull up a new loop, still keeping the base stitch on the left-hand needle.

Step 4: Bring yarn to the front of the work, creating a yarnover as the second stitch of your final five.

Step 5: Knit into the base stitch again, creating the third stitch.

Step 6: Bring yarn to the front of the work a second time, creating a yarnover that will be your fourth stitch.

Step 7: Knit into the base stitch once more, making 5 stitches created from the single base stitch on the row below.

Pkok (Pass Stitch, Knit, over, Knit) aka Mock Cable with Eyelet

This technique, worked over 3 stitches, looks almost like a cable, but is worked without traditional cabling techniques. The single eyelet in the middle gives it an openness and delicacy that traditional cables lack.

It is most often seen in Japanese stitch patterns.

Step 1: Work to the 3 stitches that will become the pkok, leaving them on the left-hand needle.

Step 2: Pick up the third stitch of the three with your right hand needle (the one farthest from the end of the left needle).

Step 3: Pass this third stitch over the other two and drop it off the end of the left-hand needle.

Step 4: Knit the next stitch, yarn over.

Step 5: Knit the second of the remaining stitches.

BLOCKING

If you don't have blocking wires, you can use cotton crochet thread instead. If you are using cotton, thread the cotton through the straight edges before you soak the garment. It may help to tie slip knots in the ends of your blocking strings to help you pin them taut. Otherwise, follow the same blocking instructions no matter which method you are using.

Step 1: Soak your finished piece in cool water with a rinse-free wool wash. Remove it gently from the water, squeezing out excess water, but being careful not to wring the fabric. Lay it out on a towel, then roll up the towel and the knitting together to soak up excess water.

Thread blocking wires through straight edges every half-inch or so. Find a clean space large enough to fit the whole piece unhindered. If a carpeted floor doesn't work you can pin it to the top of a bed, or foam tiles or a rug placed on a hard floor.

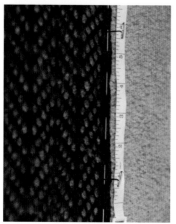

Step 2: Place pins along straight edges every 6" or so. While you are pinning, if the straight edges bow between the pins, then add more pins to keep the edge straight.

Use the tape measure or a yardstick to ensure that you keep the wires straight as you pin out the first edge.

Step 3: Take a look along the straight edge and make any adjustments to ensure that the edge is straight. Look down the length; it should be clear if you have bowed portions of the straight line.

Even with curved edges, making slight adjustments to the line of pins will be necessary. You can also change the pin placement to ensure that your fabric is as taut as possible.

Step 4: From the straight line, measure outward to the finished measurements and pin the other edges to the appropriate size.

For a triangular shawl, pin the bottom point to the right measurement then.

Step 5: Pin along edges, keeping measurements even across the whole piece. If your first straight edge was even, and you pin the other edge to the same measurement from the first edge, then the second edge should be parallel to the first.

Step 6: When picots are built in to the edge stitches, place a pin in the point, stretch it out, and pin it down.

Non-straight edges can also be made into soft scallops. Place more than one pin along the edge of the scallop to make a softer point.

To block curved lines, prepare knitting as instructed in Step 1. Place pins on the inside of the curve to hold the blocking wires in place. With curved lines you will need frequent readjusting to get an even curve. Cotton thread doesn't work as well for curved lines as blocking wires do, and you need a blocking wire with enough flexibility and tensile strength to make the curve without buckling into an odd angle.

It can help to place one pin along the outside of the curve as an anchor to keep the blocking wire ends curving in the right direction.

When you need to use multiple blocking wires to span a distance, thread both wires together through a few inches of the fabric (as seen near the left-most pin). For a curved line, you can use one of the previous pins along the curve as an anchor pin, just flip the end of the blocking wire over the anchor pin to the inside of the curve (as seen on the right-most pin).

You can also use a wire to pull out a series of picots either on a curved or a straight line. Just thread the wire through the most extreme point of the picot, then pin the wire taut.

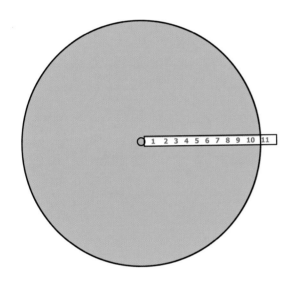

When you're blocking a circle (or a shawl with a circular outer edge, like Lune), pin the zero end of your tape measure down in the center of the circle and extend the other end out toward the circle's outer edge. You can rotate your tape measure completely around the circle like the hands of a clock. If you place your pins at exactly the same distance from the center, then you will end up with a perfect circular outer edge.

THE
PATTERNS

The main leafy motif in this piece makes a great scalloped edge and is deceptively easy to work. When worked with an alpaca blend yarn (as in the wrap version), it drapes and swings in an alluring way reminiscent of diagonal pleats.

DROPLEAF WRAP

CONSTRUCTION

Whether scarf or wrap, this piece is knitted from one cast on short edge along the full length of the piece. To get the most out of the yardage for the scarf, you can replace the border stitches with garter edge stitches (3 on each side) as is done with the Red/Brown version.

NOTES

• Markers are indicated on the charts by blue lines, and repeats are indicated by red boxes. Place markers where indicated when you begin Chart 1. Markers should simply be slipped when you come to them.

• It is not recommended that you use stitch markers between chart repeats (the red lines on the chart) in this pattern. You would frequently need to borrow stitches from one side of the marker to the other.

• Work the red outlined repeats as many times as indicated for the chart repeat to get across each section.

• Make sure that a marker doesn't accidentally slip past a yarn over next to it and migrate into the wrong position.

• If you are replacing the borders with garter stitch, it might be helpful to cover up the border portions of the charts with sticky notes.

PLUM VERSION

Yarn: 866 yards (2 skeins of 50 gm each) of Berroco Ultra Alpaca Fine (50% Peruvian Wool/20% Superfine Alpaca/30% Nylon) in 'Prune Mix'. 20 wpi

Needles: 3.5 mm (US 4) straight or circular needle for flat knitting or size needed to obtain gauge.

Gauge: 21 stitches and 26 rows over 4 inches (10 cm) in center pattern after blocking.

Finished Size: 20 inches (51 cm) wide, 70 inches (178 cm) long. Worked with 6 repeats for length.

RED/BROWN VERSION

Yarn: 253 yards (about 4 ounces) of handspun 2-ply from Chameleon Colorworks BFL Top (100% Blue Faced Leicester wool) in 'Briar Rose'. 11 wpi

Needles: 3.75 mm (US 5) straight or circular needle for flat knitting or size needed to obtain gauge.

Gauge: 15 stitches and 16 rows over 4 inches (10 cm) in center pattern after blocking.

Finished Size: 7 inches (18 cm) wide, 60 inches (152 cm) long. Worked with 3 repeats for length.

Notions: 2 stitch markers, tapestry needle to weave in ends.

With lace borders: Cast on multiples of 13 sts plus 40. The wrap has a 105 st cast-on (5 repeats of 13 sts plus 40).
With garter borders: Cast on multiples of 13 sts plus 20. The scarf has a 33 st cast-on (1 repeat of 13 sts plus 20).

Knit 3 rows.

Work Rows 1-78 of Chart 1 until desired length is reached or until only 3 rows worth of yarn remain (see page 5). The scarf was worked with 3 repeats of Chart 1 and the wrap was worked with 6 repeats.

Knit 3 rows. Bind off with a knit lace bindoff (see page 22). Weave in ends and block, pinning border points out and short edges into scallops.

Chart 1

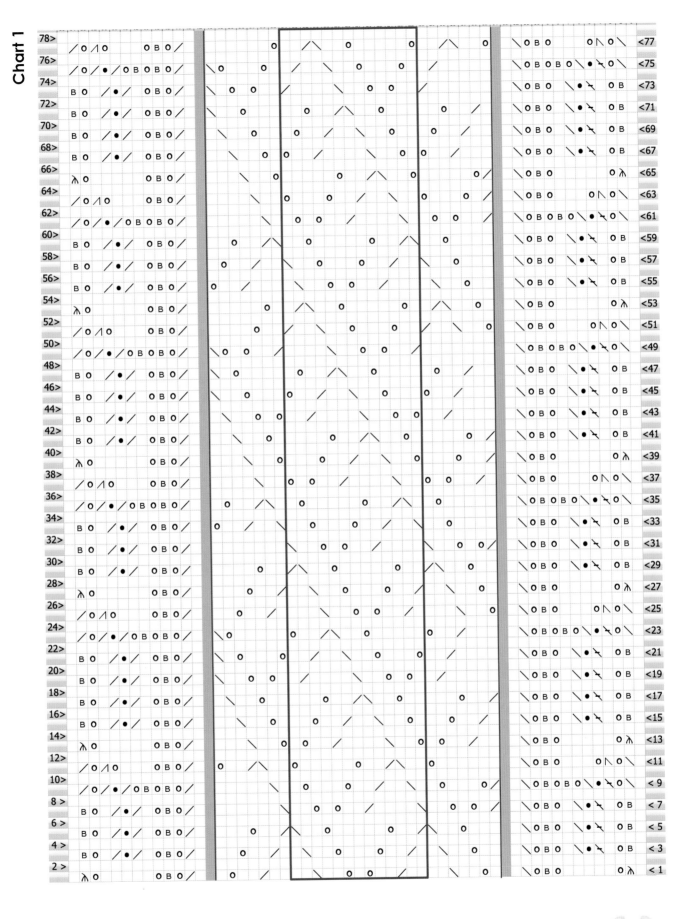

PATTERN – DROPLEAF WRAP

This shawl is the epitome of easy knitting, with top-down construction and simple eyelet rows. Worked in a heavyweight yarn, it's perfect for sitting fireside with your knitting or as an extra layer with a sweater.

Comfy Shawl

Construction

This shawl is worked from the neck down, using yarn overs on each end of each right side row to shape the "wings" and paired yarn overs in the center of each right side row (separated by a center stitch) to shape the point down the spine. These four increased stitches are added every right side row, making each row successively longer than the last, so that what started with five stitches cast on ends with substantially more.

Finish working the main color with any full row, and then work the finishing row and bind off with the contrasting color. This shawl can be worked in any weight and any amount of yarn, although needle size should be adjusted appropriately.

Notes

- Markers are indicated on the charts by blue lines, and repeats are indicated by red boxes. Markers are mentioned in the text directions when they are placed and not mentioned thereafter. They should simply be slipped when you come to them.
- Work the red outlined repeats as many times as needed to get across each section.
- For a larger or smaller shawl, increase or reduce the repeats of Chart 2.
- Make sure that a marker doesn't accidentally slip past a yarn over next to it and migrate into the wrong position. The two center markers should always be on either side of the center stitch (which is underlined), and each edge marker should be 2 stitches in from the edge of the fabric.

Green Version

Yarns: MC: 400 yards (8 ounces) of Peace Fleece Worsted (70% wool/30% mohair, 200 yards per 4 ounce skein) in 'Baikal/Superior Green' and CC: 30 yards (less than 1 skein) in 'Grassroots'. 18 wpi

Needles: 6mm (US 10) 40-inch circular or size needed to obtain gauge.

Gauge: 12 stitches and 19 rows over 4 inches (10 cm) in stockinette after blocking.

Finished Size: 72 inches (183 cm) across the top, and 36 inches (91.5 cm) from neck to bottom point.

Brown Version

Yarn: MC: 275 yards (8.5 ounces) of handspun 2-ply aran weight yarn from Spinderella's Thrums (unique composition for each batch), 9 wpi and CC: 40 yards (less than 1 skein) of Cascade Ecological Wool (100% wool) in 'Burgundy'.

Needles: 7mm (approx. US 10.75) 30-inch circular or size needed to obtain gauge.

Gauge: 9 stitches and 17 rows over 4 inches (10 cm) in stockinette after blocking.

Finished Size: 64 inches (162 cm) across the top, and 32 inches (81 cm) from neck to bottom point.

Notions: 4 stitch markers, tapestry needle to weave in ends.

Cast on 5 sts.

Rows 1 -2: Knit

Row 3: k2, yo, <u>k1</u>, yo, k2 (7 sts)

Row 4: k2, p3, k2

Row 5: k2, pm, yo, k1, yo, pm, <u>k1</u>, pm, yo, k1, yo, pm, k2. (11 sts)

Row 6: k2, purl to 2 sts from end, k2

Row 7: k2,sl m, yo, k to marker, yo, sl m, <u>k1</u>, sl m, yo, k to marker, yo, sl m, k2 (15 sts)

Row 8: k2, p to 2 sts from end, k2

Rows 9-10: repeat Rows 7 & 8 (19 sts)

Work Rows 1-14 of Chart 1 (47 sts)

Work Rows 1-16 of Chart 2 until you run out of MC yarn, ending with any full row. Each repeat of Chart 2 adds 32 sts.

<u>Contrasting Border:</u>

If you finished ready to begin a RS row:

Using CC yarn held double, k2, p to last 2 sts, k2

Bind off loosely in purl.

If you finished ready to begin a WS row:

Using CC yarn held double, knit 1 row.

Bind off loosely in knit.

Weave in ends and block.

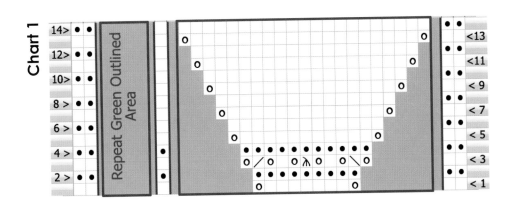

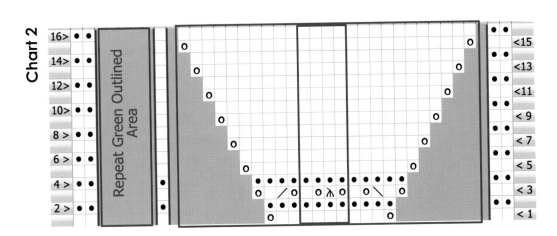

PATTERNS – COMFY SHAWL

Vinca combines the best aspects of triangular shawls
with the long, elegant wings of a rectangular stole.
It's easy to wear with clean and lovely lines.

VINCA SHAWL

CONSTRUCTION

This shawl is worked in a square from the center outward in a counterpane construction until the desired size from neck to bottom point is achieved, then two sides of the square are bound off, leaving the remaining two sides with live stitches. For Row 1 of the wings, both wings are worked together, then beginning with Row 2, those remaining two sides are then worked separately until the desired length of the wings is reached, or until the yarn runs out. Both wings may be worked simultaneously on the same needle using separate balls of yarn.

NOTES

• Markers are indicated on the charts by blue lines, and repeats are indicated by red boxes. Place markers where indicated when you begin each chart. Markers should simply be slipped when you come to them. Red lines without boxes indicate where you have added enough stitches for a full repeat.

• Work the red outlined repeats as many times as needed to get across each section.

• Make sure that a marker doesn't accidentally slip past a yarnover next to it and migrate into the wrong position. Each set of corner stitch markers should always be on either side of the corner stitch, and each edge marker should be 3 stitches in from the edge of the fabric.

• Throughout the body section, change to the longer needles when you have too many stitches to comfortably fit on the current configuration.

• To get a nice length for the wings on a scarf or shawl version, I would recommend using less than or equal to 1/5 of the total yarn for the counterpane portion, any more than that and the wings will be stubby and short in comparison (as they are for the gaiter).

• If you choose to work both wings simultaneously, it is a good idea to split the remaining yarn in half before you begin the first repeat of Row 2 of Chart 3 (see page 5)

• It may help to pin the wings together as you go to ensure you finish the same row of both wings before turning your work. This will allow you to instantly tell if you have worked the current row on both wings.

SHAWL VERSION

Yarn: 940 yards (100 grams) of Malabrigo Lace (100% Baby Merino Wool, 470 yards per 50 gram skein) in 'Cypress 20'. 18 wpi

Needles: Set of five 3.5mm (US 4) double pointed needles, 16- or 20-inch and 24-inch circular needles or size needed to obtain gauge.

Gauge: 20 stitches and 32 rows over 4 inches (10 cm) in Chart 3 repeat after blocking.

Finished Size: 50 inches (127 cm)from bottom point to end of each wing and each wing 14 inches (35 cm) wide, 20 inches (51 cm) from neck to bottom point.

GAITER VERSION

Yarn: 230 yards (4 ounces) of handspun 3-ply Superfine Merino wool from Wooly Wonka Roving in 'Desert Rose'. 14 wpi.

Needles: Set of five 3.75mm (US 5) double pointed needles, 16- or 20-inch circular or size needed to obtain gauge.

Gauge: 19 stitches and 28 rows over 4 inches (10 cm) in Chart 3 repeat after blocking.

Finished Size: 29 inches (74 cm) from bottom point to end of each wing and each wing 12 inches (30 cm) wide, 17 inches (43 cm) from neck to bottom point.

Notions: 8 stitch markers, with one being different to mark the beginning of the round, tapestry needle to weave in ends.

Counterpane:

Cast on 8 sts using Disappearing Loop method (see page 16). Distribute sts evenly on double points and join in the round, being careful not to twist. Charts 1&2 only show one side of the square. Work each row of those charts 4 times to make the whole round.

Work Rows 1-32 of Chart 1 (136 sts)
Work Rows 1-40 of Chart 2 until diagonal measurement is as desired taking care to end either with Row 20 or Row 40. Which one you finish with will determine which version of Chart 3 you use.

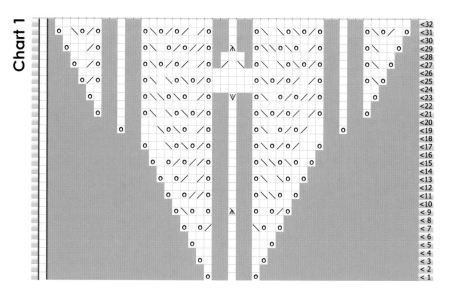

Bind off 2 sides of the square with purled lace bind off (see page 24), using the corner stitch on the second side to bind off the last stitch from the second wedge. Count the second corner stitch as one of the live stitches remaining.

Wings:

If you finished the Counterpane with Row 40, work the wings from Chart 3A. If you finished with Row 20, work the wings from Chart 3B.

Begin Row 1 of the appropriate version of Chart 3, except work the corner stitch at the end of the first wing as kfb. These 2 stitches will count as the last edge stitch of the first wing and the first edge stitch of the second wing respectively. Begin working the wings separately at this point.

Work Rows 2-20 of Chart 3A or 3B
Work Rows 1-20 of Chart 3A or 3B until the desired length is reached, or until each wing has used up half of the remaining yarn.

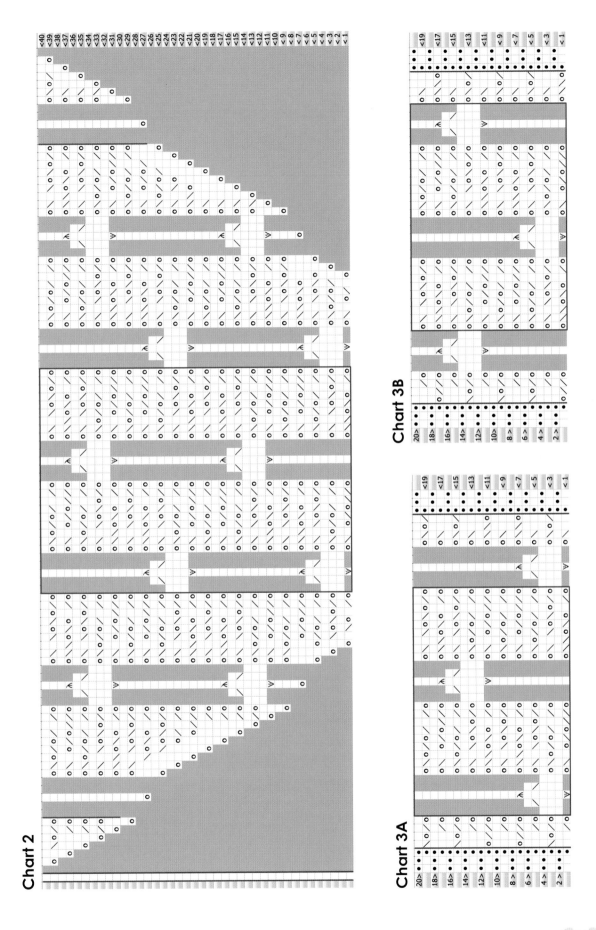

Chart 2

Chart 3B

Chart 3A

This simple zig zagging stitch motif provides the perfect canvas for a beautiful yarn. The small repeat and the easy construction make it ideal for handspun yarn as well. The width can be easily adjusted and the scarf may be bound off when you run out of yarn.

TRANSVERSE SCARF

CONSTRUCTION

This scarf is worked in one piece from one short end to the other, with increases and decreases built into the pattern to create a zigzag border that flows with the zigzag in the stitch motif. If you choose to make the scarf out of a heavier or lighter weight yarn, you can adjust the cast on and the number of repeats as instructed in the notes. The nature of the repeat means that you can cast off whenever you would like, although it would be best done either at the midpoint or the end of a repeat.

NOTES

• If you desire a shorter or longer scarf, just reduce or increase the repeats of Chart 1.

• All charts are also given with text translations of the chart. The chart legend is on the last page of this pattern.

• Two main markers are used to mark the edge stitches (the blue lines on the chart). All markers should simply be slipped when you come to them. Be sure to create the m1's inside the markers so they sit with the body stitches and not the edge stitches.

• In order to change the width of the scarf, add or subtract the number of stitches cast on by increments of 4 sts.

• If you substitute yarn and choose a fiber with more memory than silk (such as wool), it would be a good idea to double the edge stitches to keep the scarf from curling. To do this just add 4 sts to the cast on and work the edge stitches on the chart twice (i.e. on Row 1 of the chart that would be k1, p1, k1, p1).

• You may vary the length of the scarf by working a different number of repeats of the Chart, but you will need to keep a few yards in reserve for the final Border and the bindoff. This amount should be about 3-4 times the amount of yarn used in one row (see page 5).

• If you choose to make the scarf shorter or longer than instructed, I would recommend that you finish the Chart work either ending after a full repeat of the chart, or after completing Row 8 of the Chart. However, you can begin the final border and bind-off section after any completed row.

• For the recommended yarn, you need to wash it repeatedly in warm water with soap to get the sizing out of the silk. This will allow it to drape and will make the yarn more round.

BRONZE VERSION

Yarn: 352 yards (2 ounces) of Habu Textiles N-6B Konyaku Root Sizing Silk (100% silk, 88 yards per 0.5 ounce skein) in 'Copper'; 18 wpi

Needles: 3.75mm (US 5) straight or circular needles for flat knitting or size needed to obtain gauge

Gauge: 20 sts and 32 rows per 4 inches (10 cm) square in zigzag pattern after blocking

Finished Size: 10 inches (25.5 cm) wide and 70 inches (178 cm) long

Notions: 2 stitch markers, tapestry needle to weave in ends

Cast on 41 sts.

Border Row 1: k1, p1, pm, (k1, p1) to 2 last 2 sts, pm, p1, k1
Border Row 2: k1, (p1, k1) to end

Work Rows 1-16 of Chart, 30 times or until you have about 4 yards of yarn left (see notes)

Repeat **Border Row 1**.

Bind off in seed stitch as follows: K1, p1, *purl those 2 sts together. K1, knit 2 tog tbl, p1, repeat from * until all stitches are bound off. Pull end through final stitch.

Weave in ends. Wash as instructed in notes, and block, pinning out peaks on the long edges.

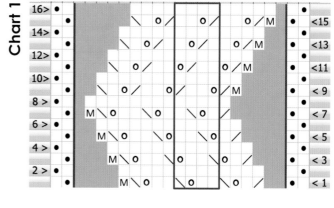

Chart 1

A simple geometric lace pattern is transformed when worked across the width of this triangular shawl. Motte means "moth" in German, and the subtle colors and winged motif would put the most beautiful moth to shame.

MOTTE SHAWL

CONSTRUCTION

This shawl is worked from one corner along the wingspan, increasing for the back point, and then decreasing again to the other corner.

NOTES

• Markers are indicated on the charts by blue lines, and repeats are indicated by red boxes. Place markers where indicated when you begin Chart 1. Markers should simply be slipped when you come to them.

• Work the red outlined repeats as many times as needed to get across each section.

• Make sure that a marker doesn't accidentally slip past a yarnover next to it and migrate into the wrong position. The two center markers should always be on either side of the center stitch, and each edge marker should be 3 stitches in from the edge of the fabric.

• You may chose to use markers to denote lace repeats, if so, place them where the red lines are on the charts.

BLUE VERSION

Yarn: 220 yards (100 grams) of Lorna's Laces Pearl (51% silk/49% bamboo, 100 grams per skein) in 'Sheridan'. 18 wpi

Needles: 5mm (US 8) circular or straight needle for flat knitting or size needed to obtain gauge.

Gauge: 20 stitches and 30 rows over 4 inches (10 cm) in stockinette after blocking.

Finished Size: 46 inches (117 cm) across the top, and 16 inches (41 cm) from neck to bottom point.

PURPLE/PINK VERSION

Yarn: 496 yards (4 ounces) of handspun single ply wool/mohair from Ethnicity Goddess Roving in 'Paradise'. 14 wpi

Needles: 4mm (US 6) circular or straight needle for flat knitting or size needed to obtain gauge.

Gauge: 15 stitches and 26 rows over 4 inches (10 cm) in stockinette after blocking

Finished Size: 60 inches (152 cm) across the top, and 22 inches (56 cm) from neck to bottom point

Notions: 2 stitch markers (more if desired, see note) tapestry needle to weave in ends.

Cast on 6 sts.
Setup Row (WS): p6

Work Rows 1-14 of Chart 1 (13 sts)
Work Rows 1-14 of Chart 2 until no less than 50% of the yarn remains, taking care to end having completed Row 8 of Chart 2.
Work Rows 1-14 of Chart 3 until only 17 sts remain.
Work Rows 1-21 of Chart 4 (6 sts)

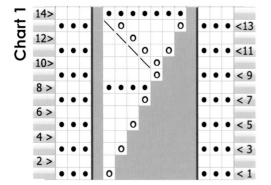

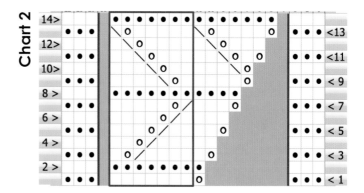

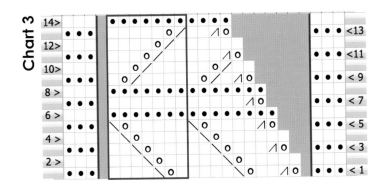

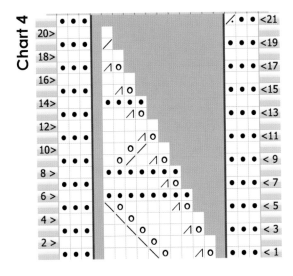

These socks are fun and easy to work in any gauge.
The lozenge pattern at the cuff and toe of these socks
reminds me of the multi-chambered cross section of
sea sponges, which have the genus name Porifera.

PORIFERA SOCKS

CONSTRUCTION

These socks are knit from the toe up. The toe starts with a provisional cast-on, followed by 6 rows of stockinette to make a little flap. You will pick up stitches around the flap (including the provisional cast on) and begin to work in the round.

The number of stitches you will need can be determined by referring to the foot circumference you would like to knit for in the Stitch Table. Negative ease (the stretch that keeps the sock on) is built in to these numbers. Try using different needle sizes to adjust your gauge to match one of the options given for your foot circumference. If your foot measurement falls between two given sizes, choose the smaller one, or use a smaller needle to tighten your gauge.

NOTES

• This pattern requires you to either split your yarn in half (50% of total yarn for each sock) or to work from both ends of a center-pull ball (see page 5).

• Treat every yo2 as two stitches. You will work (p1, k1) in each yo2 when you encounter it in the following round.

ORANGE VERSION

Yarn: 400 yards (100 grams) of Woolen Rabbit Harmony Sock Yarn (80% merino wool/20% Nylon, 100 grams per skein) in 'Red Hot Chili Peppers'; 19 wpi

Needles: Set of five 2.5 mm (US 1.5) double pointed needles, or size needed to obtain gauge.

Gauge: 18 sts and 28 rows per 2 inches (5 cm) square in stockinette.

Finished Size: Sample shown is knit with 64 sts to fit a woman's size 9. Circumference around upper cuff is 14 inches (36 cm).

Notions: Marker for beginning of round, waste yarn for provisional cast-on, tapestry needle to weave in ends.

sts/1 inch (2.5 cm)	Foot Circumference				
	7 inches	8 inches	9 inches	10 inches	11 inches
	Number of stitches in sock				
5		32			48
5.5	32			48	
6			48		64
7		48		64	
8	48		64		80
9		64		80	
9.5	64		80	80	96

Cast On Table:

# of sts In sock	# of sts to Cast On
32	8
48	10
64	12
60	16
96	20

Toe:

Using the Stitch Table above, determine how many total stitches you will have in your sock. Then, using the # of sts in your sock, determine the number of stitches to cast on using cast on Table. Provisionally cast on this number of sts (see page 14).

Purl 1 row with working yarn and 2 double pointed needles, then work 6 rows in stockinette stitch to form a small rectangle.

Open provisional cast on and transfer sts to a spare needle. Return to the live sts at the opposite end and with the working yarn and RS facing, k4 (5, 6, 8, 10) sts onto Needle 1, with an empty needle, k remaining 4 (5, 6, 8, 10) sts; pick up and knit 2 sts from side of rectangle (6 [7, 8, 10, 12] sts on Needle 2); pick up and knit 2 more sts from this side, then k 4 (5, 6, 8, 10) sts from provisional cast-on (6 [7, 8, 10, 12] sts on Needle 3); knit remaining 4 (5, 6, 8, 10) sts from provisional cast-on, pick up and knit 2 sts from remaining short side, (6 [7, 8, 10, 12] sts on Needle 4); pick up last 2 sts from this side of rectangle (do not knit them yet) and place them on Needle 1. The beginning of the round starts with Needle 1. 24 (28, 32, 40, 48) sts total.

Knit 1 round even.

Toe Rnd. 1: Needles 1 & 3: k1, m1, k to end of needle. Needles 2 & 4: k to last st, m1, k1
Toe Rnd. 2: Knit

Repeat these 2 rnds until the total # of sts for your sock (according to table) is reached. Measure lenth of toe at this point and record. Toe measures _____ inches/cm. This measurement is referred to as X.

Work 2 rnds of Instep Ribbing as follows: k1 (p2, k2) to 3 st before end of Needle 2, p2, k1. knit to end of round.

Foot:

Once Toe Chart is completed, continue in established ribbing pattern until the foot measures X inches/cm short of desired total foot length (this should be the total length of the toe as determined before beginning ribbing), ending with 1 st unknit before the end of the round.

Heel:

Note: Heel will be worked flat over needles 3 & 4 only.
Using the 1 st rem in rnd, w&t.
Short Row 1 (WS): purl to 1 st before the end of heel sts, w&t.
Short Row 2 (RS): knit to 1 st before the next wrapped stitch, w&t.
Short Row 3: purl to 1 st before the next wrapped stitch, w&t.
Repeat Short Rows 2&3 until 8(10, 12, 16, 20) sts rem unwrapped between wraps.
Short Row 4: knit to next wrapped st. Pu wrap and knit tog tbl with wrapped st, w&t.
Short Row 5: purl to next wrapped st. Pu wrap and purl tog with wrapped st, w&t.
Short Row 6: knit to next wrapped st. Pu **both** wraps & k tog tbl with wrapped st, w&t.
Short Row 7: purl to next wrapped st. Pu **both** wraps & purl tog with wrapped st, w&t.
Repeat Short Rows 6&7 until only 1 wrapped st remains on each end of heel stitches.
Short Row 8: knit to final wrapped st. Pu both wraps & k tog tbl with wrapped st, turn.
Short Row 9: purl to final wrapped st. Pu both wraps & purl tog with wrapped st, turn and mark as beginning of round, reordering needles from this point. Begin working in the round, Needles 1 and 2 will have the heel sts and needles 3 and 4 the instep.

Cuff Rnd 1: Sl1, knit to end of needle 2, pu 1 st between needles 2 & 3 and knit it together with the first stitch of needle 3. Work Needles 3 & 4 in established rib pattern until last stitch of Needle 4, pu 1 st between needle 4 & 1, ssk together with last st from needle 4.

Cuff Rnd 2: Needles 1 & 2: knit, Needles 3 & 4 work in established rib.

Repeat Cuff Rnd 2 three more times.
Cuff Rnd 3: k1, (p2, k2) to 3 sts from end of rnd, p2, k1.

Repeat Cuff Rnd 3, measuring how much yarn each round requires (see page 5) and record it here: _____ feet/yards/meters per round of cuff. Multiply this number by 50 and record it as Y. Y=_____ feet/yards/meters. For example if it took 1 yard for each round, then Y would equal 50 yards.

Work Cuff Rnd 3 until you have Y feet/yards/meters of each ball (or 2 times Y feet/yards/meters if you are working from one center-pull ball) remaining.

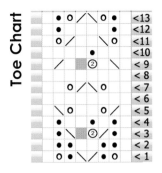

Toe Chart

Rows: <13, <12, <11, <10, <9, <8, <7, <6, <5, <4, <3, <2, <1

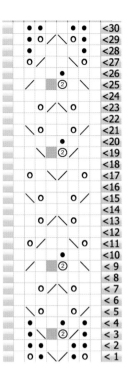

Cuff Chart

Rows: <30, <29, <28, <27, <26, <25, <24, <23, <22, <21, <20, <19, <18, <17, <16, <15, <14, <13, <12, <11, <10, <9, <8, <7, <6, <5, <4, <3, <2, <1

This shawl is named after Cleite, one of the mythical Amazons of the ancient world, who accompanied the Amazon queen, Penthesilea, to the Trojan War. Designed with a simple stitch pattern, the placement of the decreases creates a scalloped line when bound off without adding a separate edging.

CLEITE SHAWL

CONSTRUCTION

This shawl is worked from the neck down, using yarn overs on each end of each right side row to shape the "wings" and paired yarn overs in the center of each right side row (separated by a center stitch) to shape the point down the spine. These 4 increased stitches are added every right side row, making each row successively longer than the last, so that what started with 5 stitches cast on, ends with hundreds.

NOTES

•If you desire a shorter or longer shawl, just reduce or increase the repeats of Chart 2.

•All charts are also given with text transcriptions of the chart. The chart legend is on page 5 of this pattern, after the charts.

•Four main markers are used. After being placed while working Row 1 of Chart 1, the 2 markers on the ends separate the garter edge stitches on each side of the shawl from the body, and the two in the middle flank the center stitch. Markers are mentioned when they are placed, and not mentioned thereafter. They should simply be slipped when you come to them. You may choose to place stitch markers to denote lace repeats (the red boxes on the chart). If you choose this option, please refer to the next note.

•If you use stitch markers to mark lace repeats, at the beginning of every repeat of Chart 2 you will need to shift these repeat markers and add new markers to denote new repeats as you increase the number of stitches in the row. The first time you knit Chart 2, you will work the red boxed repeat 1 time. For the second time you knit Chart 2, you will work the red boxed repeat 2 times across the row, etc....

RED VERSION

Yarn: 1 skein of Sundara Silk Lace (100% silk, 1000 yds per 100 gm skein), in 'Sangria over Garnet'; 26 wpi

Needles: 3.25mm (US 3) 24- to 30-inch circular neelde or size needed to obtain gauge

Gauge: 22 sts over 4 inches (10 cm) in stockinette after blocking. Since length is variable, row gauge is less important.

Finished Size: 80 inches (203 cm) across the top and 40 inches (102 cm) from neck to point

Notions: 4 stitch markers (more if desired, see notes), tapestry needle to weave in ends

Cast on 5 sts using a cable cast on and knit 2 rows.

Row 1: k1, kf&b, k1, kf&b, k1 (7 sts).
Row 2: k2, p3, k2.

Work Rows 1-24 of Chart 1, placing markers where indicated. (55 sts total)
Work Rows 1-24 of Chart 2, 9 times or until desired length is reached.

Once repeats of Chart 2 are complete, bind off using knitted lace bind off (see page 22)

Weave in ends and block, pinning out scallops along bound off edge.

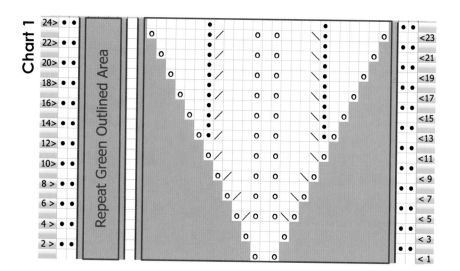

Chart 2

PATTERNS – CLEITE SHAWL

The graceful crescent shape of this shawl makes it most comfortable to wear and a lot of fun to knit. The inner curve of the crescent allows the shawl to hang effortlessly from the shoulders while creating a delicate fluttering tail edge.

Lune Shawl

Construction

This shawl begins with a provisional cast on, from which a small flap of garter stitch is knit. Stitches are then picked up from the side of the flap and the provisional cast on, then the shawl is worked from the back of the neck outward to the long circular edge in the same manner as a traditional top-down triangular shawl, but with a different increase structure. Each right side row has six increases (one at each edge and four more spaced across the row), and each wrong side row has two increases just inside the edge stitches totaling eight stitches increased every two rows. This rapid rate of increase is what forms the crescent shape of the shawl.

These increase points create several distinct sections into which lace patterns have been inserted for the red version- the center panel with the lozenge motif, the side panels with the zig-zag motif, and the edges which have been left in stockinette stitch. The lozenge motif has patterning only on right side rows, while the zig-zag motif has increases and decreases on both right and wrong sides. The purple version was knit using the Stockinette only charts, using the same increase structure, but without lace patterning.

Notes

• If you are using stitch markers for lace repeats on Chart 2, on Rows 3, 5, 11 & 13, you will have to 'borrow' stitches from the other side of the marker to complete the decrease. In Chart 2, on Rows 3 & 11, the decrease should be worked as follows: slip 1 stitch, remove marker, transfer slipped stitch back to the left hand needle, replace marker, ssk, and continue on. In Chart 2, on Rows 5 & 13, the decrease should be worked as follows: slip 1 stitch, remove marker, transfer slipped stitch back to the left hand needle, k2tog, replace marker and continue on.

• Work the red outlined repeats as many times as indicated for the chart repeat to get across each section.

• Make sure that a marker doesn't accidentally slip past a yarn over next to it and migrate into the wrong position.

• Stockinette Only charts are also given if you prefer to either add your own lace or cable pattern, or to keep the shawl very simple.

• Red lines without a box mark where you have added enough stitches for another full repeat.

Red Version

Yarn: 800 yards (about 160 grams) of Spritely Goods Sylph (100% superwash merino wool, 560 yards per 115 gram skein) in 'Cranberry'. 18 wpi

Needles: 3.5mm (US 4) 36-inch circular needle for flat knitting or size needed to obtain gauge.

Gauge: 20 stitches and 32 rows over 4 inches (10 cm) in stockinette after blocking.

Finished Size: 48 inches (122 cm) across widest point of circle, 23 inches (59 cm) from neck to bottom and 14 inches (36 cm) between upper points.

Purple Version

Yarn: 245 yards (4 ounces) of handspun 2-ply 50% merino/50% silk top from Spirit Trail Fiberworks in 'Lilac'. 11 wpi

Needles: 6mm (US 10) 36-inch circular needle for flat knitting or size needed to obtain gauge.

Gauge: 13 stitches and 16 rows over 4 inches (10 cm) in stockinette after blocking.

Finished Size: 34 inches (86 cm) across widest point of circle, 16 inches (41 cm) from neck to bottom and 6 inches (15 cm) between upper points.

Notions: 4 stitch markers (more if desired, see note) tapestry needle to weave in ends, waste yarn for provisional cast on.

With waste yarn, provisionally cast on 3 sts (see page 14). Switch to main yarn, k3. Knit 6 rows (3 garter ridges)

Set-up Row 1 (RS): k3, yo, pick up & knit 1 st from each garter ridge (3 sts total picked up and knit from the side of flap), yo, unzip provisional cast-on and knit those 3 sts, turn. (11 sts total)
Set-up Row 1 (WS): k3, yo, p5, yo, k3 (13 sts total)

Work Rows 1-8 of Chart 1 (45 sts total)
Work Rows 1-16 of Chart 2 as written with no repeats of sections A, B, C, D, or E
Work Rows 1-16 of Chart 2 again repeating A 3 times, B 5 times, C 3 times, D 5 times, and E 3 times.

Continue repeating Rows 1-16 of Chart 2, adding 2 repeats each of sections A, C & E and 4 repeats of sections B & D. For example, on the 3rd repeat of Chart 2, work A, C & E 5 times each and B & D 9 times each.

Continue with Chart 2 as set until the desired length is reached, or you have enough yarn remaining for 8 rows (see page 5 for how to calculate how much yarn you are using in a row).

Knit 4 rows (2 garter ridges). Bind off with a knitted lace bindoff (see page 22). Weave in ends and block pinning the outside edge as close to a perfect circle as possible.

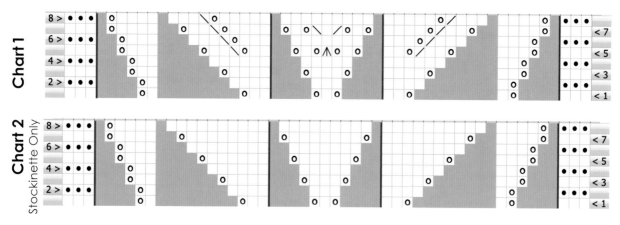

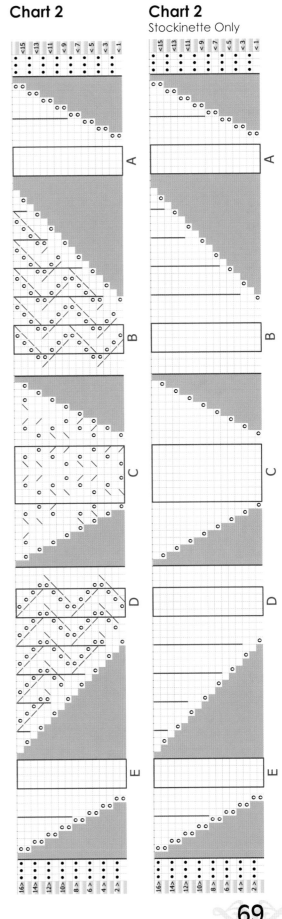

Chart 2

Chart 2
Stockinette Only

PATTERNS – LUNE SHAWL

The repeating diamond motif in this stole is like the simple
leaded glass windows popular in Tudor England. The trend
away from intricate stained glass was a turn toward
simplicity common to the Protestant Reformation.

TUDOR STOLE

CONSTRUCTION

This shawl is worked from one short edge the full length of the piece. It would be quite easy to modify this pattern wider to make a wider stole or narrower into a scarf.

NOTES

• Markers are indicated on the charts by blue lines, and repeats are indicated by red boxes. Place markers where indicated when you begin Chart 1. Markers should simply be slipped when you come to them.

• Work the red outlined repeats as many times as needed to get across each section.

• Make sure that a marker doesn't accidentally slip past a yarnover next to it and migrate into the wrong position. Each edge marker should be 4 stitches in from the edge of the fabric.

• If you are using stitch markers for every repeat, every time a double decrease is next to a stitch marker, you will have to 'borrow' stitches from the other side of the marker to complete the decrease. For instance, in Chart 1, Row 13, the decrease should be worked as follows: slip 2 sts to left hand needle, remove marker, transfer slipped stitch back to the left hand needle, work decrease, replace marker.

• The finished width can be adjusted easily by changing the number of repeats you cast on and the length can be adjusted by changing the number of repeats of Chart 1, Rows 53-56. Please be aware that your yardage will vary as you modify the pattern.

• At the beginning of Chart 3 the stitch count will change. Each repeat increases to 14 stitches for the remainder of the piece.

BLUE VERSION

Yarn: 1300 yards (about 9 ounces) of handspun 3-ply yarn from Spunky Eclectic Panda roving (60% superwash Merino, 30% bamboo, 10% nylon) in 'Blue Moon'. 24 wpi

Needles: 4.0 mm (US 6) circular or straight needle for flat knitting or size needed to obtain gauge.

Gauge: 16 stitches and 22 rows over 4 inches (10 cm) in stockinette after blocking.

Finished Size: 24 inches (61 cm) wide, and 123 inches (312 cm) long.

Notions: 2 stitch markers (more if desired, see note) tapestry needle to weave in ends.

Weigh total yarn and make note here: _____ grams.

Cast on repeats of 12 sts plus 21 for edges and borders using a long tail cast on over two needles (see page 12). Sample is done with a cast on of 93 sts (6 repeats of 12 sts, plus 21 sts)

Purl 4 rows.
Work Rows 1-2 of Chart 1 eight times
Work Rows 3-12 of Chart 1
Work Rows 13-16 of Chart 1 three times
Work Rows 17-30 of Chart 1
Work Rows 31-46 of Chart 1 twice
Work Rows 47-52 of Chart 1

Determine how much yarn is used for the border by weighing yarn now. Subtract current weight from total weight. Border weight: _____ grams.
Work Rows 53-56 of Chart 1 until only border weight of yarn remains, or until desired length minus border is reached.

Work Rows 1-14 of Chart 2
Work Rows 15-30 of Chart 2 twice
Work Rows 31-36 of Chart 2 once
Work Rows 37-40 of Chart 2 three times
Work Rows 41-46 of Chart 2
Work Rows 1-2 of Chart 3
Work Rows 3-4 of Chart 3 eight times

Purl 4 rows and bind off in purled lace bind off (see page 24). Weave in ends and block, pinning the short side points out.

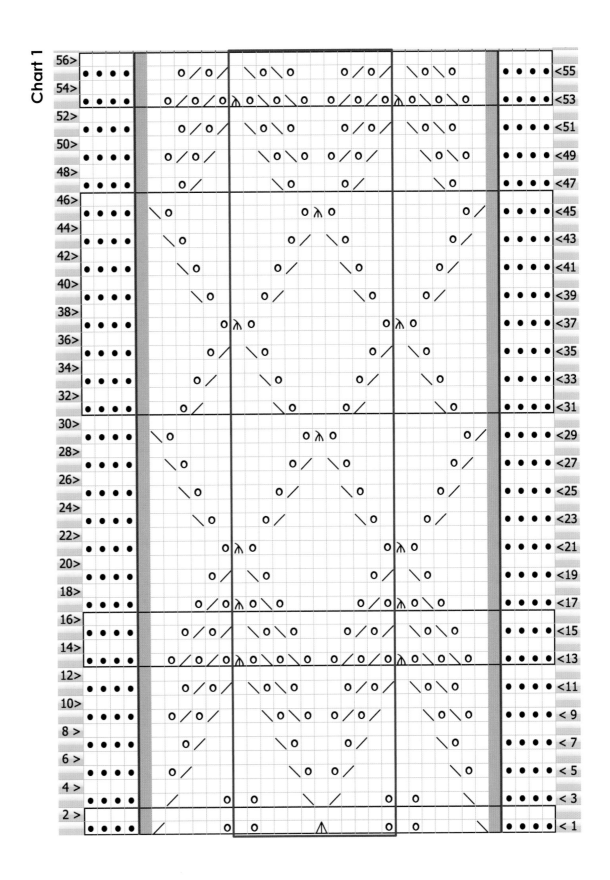

Chart 2

46> • • • •   o ⅄ o   o ⅄ o   • • • • <45
44> • • • •   o ╱   ╲ o   o ╱   ╲ o   • • • • <43
42> • • • •   o ╱ o ⅄ o ╲ o   o ╱ o ⅄ o ╲ o   • • • • <41
40> • • • •   o ╱ o ╱   ╲ o ╲ o   o ╱ o ╱   ╲ o ╲ o   • • • • <39
38> • • • •   o ╱ o ╱ o ⅄ o ╲ o ╲ o   o ╱ o ╱ o ⅄ o ╲ o ╲ o   • • • • <37
36> • • • •   o ╱ o ╱   ╲ o ╲ o   o ╱ o ╱   ╲ o ╲ o   • • • • <35
34> • • • •   o ╱ o ╱   ╲ o ╲ o   o ╱ o ╱   ╲ o ╲ o   • • • • <33
32> • • • •   o ╱   ╲ o   o ╱   ╲ o   • • • • <31
30> • • • •   ╲ o   o ⅄ o   o ╱   • • • • <29
28> • • • •   ╲ o   o ╱   ╲ o   o ╱   • • • • <27
26> • • • •   ╲ o   o ╱   ╲ o   o ╱   • • • • <25
24> • • • •   ╲ o   o ╱   ╲ o   o ╱   • • • • <23
22> • • • •   o ⅄ o   o ⅄ o   • • • • <21
20> • • • •   o ╱   ╲ o   o ╱   ╲ o   • • • • <19
18> • • • •   o ╱   ╲ o   o ╱   ╲ o   • • • • <17
16> • • • •   o ╱   ╲ o   o ╱   ╲ o   • • • • <15
14> • • • •   ╲ o   o ⅄ o   o ╱   • • • • <13
12> • • • •   ╲ o   o ╱   ╲ o   o ╱   • • • • <11
10> • • • •   ╲ o   o ╱   ╲ o   o ╱   • • • • < 9
8 > • • • •   ╲ o   o ╱   ╲ o   o ╱   • • • • < 7
6 > • • • •   o ⅄ o   o ⅄ o   • • • • < 5
4 > • • • •   o ╱   ╲ o   o ╱   ╲ o   • • • • < 3
2 > • • • •   o ╱ o ⅄ o ╲ o   o ╱ o ⅄ o ╲ o   • • • • < 1

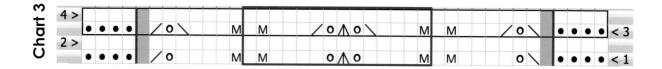

Chart 3

4 > • • • •   ╱ o ╲   M   M   ╱ o ⅄ o ╲   M   M   ╱ o ╲   • • • • < 3
2 > • • • •   ╱ o   M   M   o ⅄ o   M   M   o ╲   • • • • < 1

Nothing beats a cowl as an extra layer under a winter coat or as the perfect spring accessory when the days are getting longer. Twisting lace and cable motifs strike a nice balance of beauty and warmth.

WINDWARD COWL

CONSTRUCTION

This cowl is worked in the round from the bottom edge, decreasing to form a flared base to fit around the shoulders. The cowl is continued until you either run out of yarn or the desired length is reached.

Instructions are given for two sizes – 18 inches unpinned and 24 inches unpinned. For each of these target circumferences, use the cast-on number given for your gauge in the table. If your gauge does not precisely match the gauge in the table, adjustments to the final circumference can be made during blocking.

NOTES

• Work each chart as many times as needed to finish the round.

• For a cast on number not on the table, or if your desired finished circumference is between 18 and 24 inches, cast on a multiple of 25 stitches between the two cast on numbers given.

• This cowl is knit in the round so every round is a RS round. Read all chart rows from Right to Left.

Cast On Table:		
sts/1 inch (2.5 cm)	18" circ	24" circ
3	75	100
4	100	125
5	125	175
6	150	200
7	175	225
8	200	275

GRAY VERSION

Yarn: 180 yards (2 ounces) of Green Mountain Spinnery New Mexico Organic (100% fine wool, 2 ounces per skein) in Natural Gray; 18 wpi

Needles: 4.5mm (US 7) 16-inch circular or size needed to obtain gauge.

Gauge: 24 stitches and 28 rows over 4 inches (10 cm) in Chart 2 relaxed after blocking.

Finished Size: Pinned out to 21 inches circumference (53 cm) at top and flared to 29 inches (73 cm) at base. When unpinned, the piece relaxes to 18 inches (46 cm) flared to 26 inches (66 cm) at base.

BURGUNDY VERSION

Yarn: 283 yards (4 ounces) of handspun Spunky Eclectic BFL Roving (100% Blue-faced Leicester wool) in 'Red Maple'; 12 wpi

Needles: 4.5mm (US 7) 16-inch circular or size needed to obtain gauge.

Gauge: 20 stitch and 25 rows over 4 inches (10 cm) in Chart 2 relaxed after blocking.

Finished Size: Pinned out to 27 inches circumference (69 cm) at top and flared to 34 inches (86 cm) at base. When unpinned, the piece relaxes to 24 inches (61 cm) flared to 32 inches (81 cm) at base.

Notions: cable needle if desired, stitch marker, tapestry needle to weave in ends.

Cast on the indicated number of stitches based on your gauge and desired circumference, using a long-tail cast on over both ends of the circular needle, or two needles held together (see page 12). Once the correct number of sts is cast on, remove the extra needle.

Join for working in the round, being careful not to twist cast-on stitches. Pm to indicated beginning of round.

Work Rnds 1-16 of Chart 1 once.

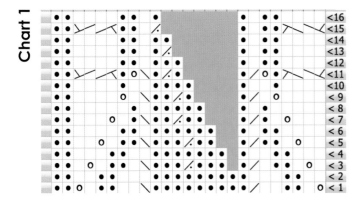

Chart 2

<32
<31
<30
<29
<28
<27
<26
<25
<24
<23
<22
<21
<20
<19
<18
<17
<16
<15
<14
<13
<12
<11
<10
< 9
< 8
< 7
< 6
< 5
< 4
< 3
< 2
< 1

Either as a scarf or a wrap, this piece is stunning.
With an easy-to-remember repeat, it would be
great travel knitting.

Colonnade Scarf

Construction

This scarf is worked beginning with the first border piece, stitches are then picked up on the edge and the length of the scarf worked perpendicular to the border. The final border is knitted on to the live stitches from the scarf.

This scarf could easily be widened into a stole by adding repeats of Chart 1 and the corresponding number of repeats across the width of the scarf.

Notes

• Markers are indicated on the charts by blue lines, and repeats are indicated by red boxes. Place markers where indicated at beginning of each chart.

• If you desire a shorter or longer scarf, just reduce or increase the repeats of Chart 2.

• All stitches bound off (including in Rows 10 & 20 of Charts 1 & 3) should be bound off as if to knit.

• Two main markers are used to mark the edge stitches (the blue lines on the chart). All markers should simply be slipped when you come to them.

• Each p2tog worked on the wrong sides of Chart 3 should join one edging stitch together with one body stitch. This binds off the body stitches at the same time it is attaching the edging perpendicular to the body.

• Pick up a stitch by inserting needle through the existing fabric and pulling working yarn through to the right side, forming a loop. Loops are then placed on the needle.

• Treat every yo2 as two stitches in the next row. You will work (p1, k1) in each yo2 when you encounter it in the following row.

Teal Version

Yarn: 350 yards (about 2.5 ounces) of Red Rocks Fiber Works Steamboat (51% silk/49% Superfine Merino, 665 yards in 5.5 ounce skein) in 'Turtlecoy'; 17 wpi

Needles: 4mm (US 6) straight or circular needles for flat knitting or size needed to obtain gauge

Gauge: 20 sts and 32 rows per 4 inches (10 cm) square in zigzag body pattern after blocking

Finished Size: 10 inches (25.5 cm) wide and 70 inches (178 cm) long

Notions: 2 stitch markers, tapestry needle to weave in ends

First Edging:

Cast on 35 sts loosely using a cable cast-on.

Knit 2 rows.

Work Rows 1-20 of Chart 1 three times (or more if you are widening the scarf into a wrap).

Knit 1 row.

Bind off loosely, leaving 1 loop remaining. Make loop large and remove needle. At this point, weigh the edging to determine how much yarn will be required for the other edging. Record it here _____ grams.

Slip whole ball of yarn through remaining loop and pull snug. Do not cut yarn.

Body:

Working from the bound-off edge toward the cast-on edge along the side of knitting with the slipped stitches, pick up 10 sts per repeat of Chart 1, plus 4 sts for border. (i.e. if you did 3 repeats of Chart 1, then pick up 34 sts: 3 repeats x 10 sts = 30 + 4 edge stitches = 34 sts total).

Work Rows 1-20 of Chart 2 until desired length is reached or until you have at least enough yarn remaining to complete the other border. End your repeats of Chart 2 having completed either Row 10 or Row 20. The Sample was knit with 24 repeats of Chart 2.

Knit 1 row; do not bind off. Leave stitches live on the needle.

Second Edging:

Using the working yarn and a cable cast-on, cast on 35 sts loosely using a cable cast-on.

K35 sts, turn. This will leave you right between the newly cast on edge stitches and the body stitches. As you work Chart 3, you will join one border stitch to one body stitch at the end of each WS row by purling the two stitches together.

Work Rows 1-20 of Chart 3 three times or until all the body stitches have been joined together with the newly created border.

Knit 1 row.

Bind off all rem stitches loosely. Cut yarn and pull through final loop. Weave in end and block, pinning border points out.

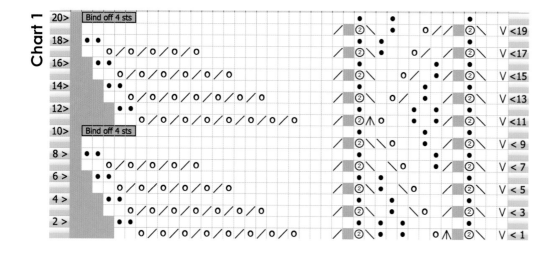

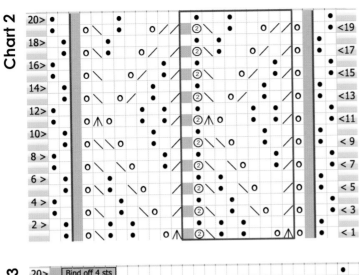

Chart 2

Rows (left): 20>, 18>, 16>, 14>, 12>, 10>, 8>, 6>, 4>, 2>
Rows (right): <19, <17, <15, <13, <11, < 9, < 7, < 5, < 3, < 1

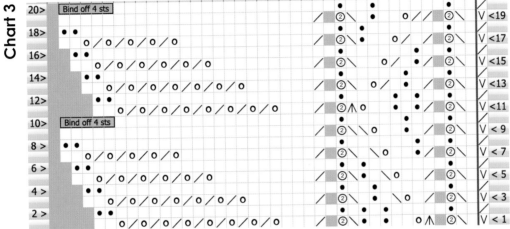

Chart 3

Rows (left): 20>, 18>, 16>, 14>, 12>, 10>, 8>, 6>, 4>, 2>
Rows (right): <19, <17, <15, <13, <11, < 9, < 7, < 5, < 3, < 1

Bind off 4 sts

Bind off 4 sts

These dainty mitts use a cabled chevron design to accentuate the wrist. Knit them as long as you like for a night at the opera or to keep your arms warm under a dress coat. The matching chevron thumb adds a touch of whimsy.

GABLE MITTS

CONSTRUCTION

These fingerless mitts begin with a decorative double stranded, double-start cast-on (see page 18). You cast on for the portion closest to the fingers. Placement of increases and decreases create the peak at the finger opening.

You will provisionally cast on the thumb gusset stitches and add them into the round when you reach the appropriate point. The thumb gusset can be placed on the palm, or between the stockinette palm and the patterned mitt back, depending on your thumb placement preference. The provisionally cast on stitches are decreased down to create the gusset.

At the wrist the chevron shaping ceases and begins to be knit straight (which pulls the wrist in and makes it snug). The arm is bound off with the stretchy sewn bind-off that when worked with a double strand of yarn approximates the cast-on edge.

NOTES

• This pattern requires you to either split your yarn in half (50% of total yarn for each mitt) or to work from both ends of a center-pull ball.

• You will need to keep about 6-7 yards (5.5-6.5 meters) of yarn in reserve for the thumbs and their bind offs. If you plan to knit the mitt cuffs until you run out of yarn, it would be a good idea to set aside this length before you cast on.

• Adjust needle and yarn size to fit a larger or smaller circumference hand. As you increase hand circumference increase the amount of yarn set aside for thumbs.

• These mitts are knit in the round so every round is a RS round. Read all chart rows from Right to Left.

ROSE VERSION

Yarn: 1 skein (200 yards per 50 grams) of The Fibre Company Canopy Fingering (50% baby alpaca/30% Merino/20% Bamboo) in 'Kafir Plum'; 17 wpi

Needles: Set of five 2.75 mm (US 2) double pointed needles, or size needed to obtain gauge.

Gauge: 16 sts and 20 rows per 2 inches (5 cm) square in stockinette.

Finished Size: To fit a 7-inch (18 cm) circumference hand. 13 inches (33 cm) from peak to cuff, worked with 4 repeats of Chart 4.

Notions: marker for beginning of round, 2 markers for thumb gusset, tapestry needle to weave in ends, waste yarn for provisional cast on.

Cast on 52 sts with the Double Stranded Double-Start Cast On (see page 18). Join for knitting in the round, being careful not to twist stitches.

P1 (k14, p1) 12 times, k to end of rnd.

K25 for palm, then work Rnd 1 of Chart 1 for back of hand.

Work Rnds 1-18 of Chart 1 in this manner, knitting the 25 palm sts and then working the appropriate rnd of Chart 1.

The thumb is cast on separately as follows: Using a provisional cast on (see page 14) cast on 16 sts onto an empty needle. As you work the next round, insert the 16 sts of the thumb gusset in the appropriate place based on your thumb placement preference. You may need to adjust the placement of needles in the round to accommodate the extra 16 stitches until a few rounds of thumb gusset decreases have been worked.

If you prefer thumb placement to be on the side of the hand, insert the thumb between the palm stitches and the back-of-hand stitches. For Right Hand Mitt, k25, pm, knit thumb gusset stitches, pm, Work Rnd 1 of Chart 2. For Left Hand Mitt, k25, Work Rnd 1 of Chart 2, pm, knit thumb gusset stitches. Use the beginning of rnd marker to also mark the end of thumb gusset sts.

If you prefer thumb placement to be on the palm of the hand, For Right Hand Mitt, k20, pm, knit thumb gusset stitches, pm, k5, Work Rnd 1 of Chart 2. For Left Hand Mitt, k5, pm, knit thumb gusset stitches, pm, k20, Work Rnd 1 of Chart 2. **Work Rnds 2-24 of Chart 2** on the back-of-hand stitches, knitting all non-gusset palm stitches, while at the same time working the thumb gusset as follows on the corresponding rows:

R2-4: knit
R5: k2tog, k12, ssk
R6-7: knit
R8: k2tog, k10, ssk
R9-10: knit

R11: k2tog, k8, ssk
R12-13: knit
R14: k2tog, k6, ssk
R15-16: knit
R17: k2tog, k4, ssk
R18-19: knit
R20: k2tog, k2, ssk
R21-22: knit
R23: k2tog, ssk
R24: k2tog

Work Rnds 1-28 of Chart 3 on back-of-hand stitches, working palm stitches in stockinette as established.

Work Rnds 1-12 of Chart 4 as established until only 6 rounds of yarn remain for each mitt (not including the yardage set aside for thumbs), making sure to work the final round replacing the stockinette on the palm side with k1 p1 ribbing to keep the edge from curling.

Bind off all cuff stitches using the Stretchy Sewn Bind off (see page 26) with yarn held double.

Thumb:
Pick up 16 sts from the provisional thumb cast on. Pick up 3 stitches from the gap where the provisional cast on ends meet and place those 3 sts on the needle closest to the patterned back of each mitt. For the Right hand, begin working the thumb rounds with the 3 gap stitches. For the left hand, end the thumb rounds with the 3 gap stitches. Attach half of the reserved thumb yarn and work thumb as follows:

Thumb Rnd 1: knit
Thumb Rnd 2: k4, ssk, k3, m1, k1, m1, k3, k2tog, k4

Repeat Thumb Rnds 1-2 four more times, then Thumb Rnd 1 once more.

Bind off all thumb stitches using the Stretchy Sewn Bind off (see page 26) with yarn held double.

Weave in ends and block.

Chart 1

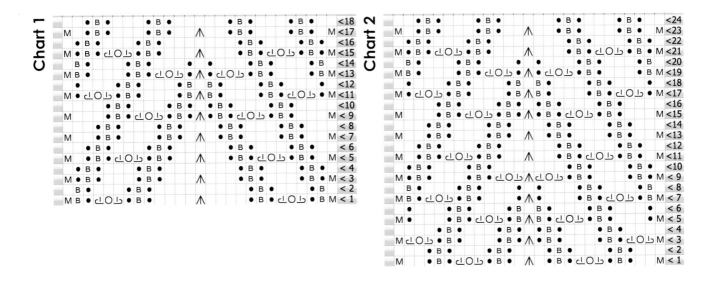

Chart 2

PATTERN – GABLE MITTS

Chart 3

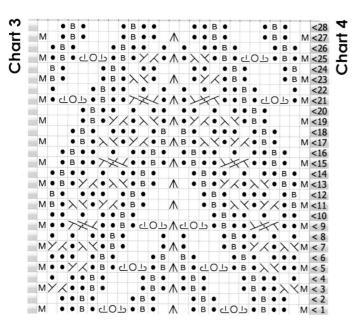

Chart 4

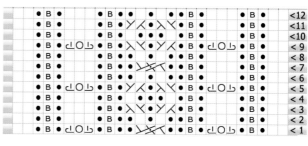

PATTERN – GABLE MITTS

About the Author

Designer Miriam Felton started playing with fiber, yarn and thread as soon as she could hold a needle. In 1999, she began knitting. Designing knitwear followed soon after. While many of her designs focus on lace patterns, all of her work features textural details, and exploring positive and negative space with the use of knitted stitches to create lyrical and strikingly visual patterns.

Miriam has had designs published in Interweave Press magazines and books, the on-line magazines Knitty and Twist Collective, the book Sensual Knits, as well as self-publishing patterns via her website at http://www.mimknits.com.

She lives in Salt Lake City with the love of her life and a rescued seal point Siamese named Ekho. This is her first book.